Feast Days & Holy Days
Color-By-Number Book

Written by
Mary Elizabeth Tebo, FSP and
Kathryn James Hermes, FSP

Illustrated by Teresa Mossi

Pauline
BOOKS & MEDIA
BOSTON

Nihil Obstat:
Rev. Timothy J. Shea

Imprimatur:
†Bernard Cardinal Law
April 1, 1999

Printed and published in the U.S.A. by Pauline Books & Media, 50 Saint Pauls Avenue, Boston, MA 02130-3491.

www.pauline org

Pauline Books & Media is the publishing house of the Daughters of St. Paul, an international congregation of women religious serving the Church with the communications media.

1 2 3 4 5 6   04 03 02 01 00 99

Some Special Days...

Each year that we spend worshiping and loving God together has a special name. It is called a *liturgical year.* During the liturgical year, we remember different times in the life of Jesus. We also celebrate special days in honor of Jesus, Mary and the saints.

This coloring book will teach you about some of these days.

We call some celebrations *feast days.* Others are called *holy days of obligation.* A holy day of obligation is a feast day that all Catholics are called to celebrate by taking part in the Eucharist (going to Mass). Joining together at Mass, we praise, adore and thank God for all the wonderful and good things he does for us.

Every Sunday of the year is a holy day of obligation. Other holy days are celebrated according to the needs of the people and the decision of the bishops in each country*

In this coloring book you will find pictures for many of the days we celebrate together as God's people. There is also something special about these pictures. They are made to look like *stained glass windows.* About 900 years ago, people began decorating their churches with windows made of brightly colored pieces of glass called *stained glass.* The windows showed scenes from the Bible and the lives of Jesus and Mary. By looking at the windows, the people could learn many things about God and his plan of salvation for the whole world.

Today stained glass windows can still be found in some churches. And if you color the following pages carefully, you can make some beautiful stained glass pictures of your very own!

---

*Unless otherwise designated by the bishop of a diocese, the holy days of obligation in the United States are:

Mary, Mother of God—January 1 (except when it falls on a Saturday or Monday)

Ascension of Our Lord—forty days after Easter, or in some western dioceses, the following Sunday

Assumption of the Blessed Virgin Mary—August 15 (except when it falls on a Saturday or Monday)

All Saints' Day—November 1 (except when it falls on a Saturday or Monday)

Mary's Immaculate Conception—December 8

Christmas—December 25

Unless otherwise designated, the holy days of obligation in Canada are:

Mary, Mother of God—January 1

Christmas—December 25

Color Key

1–apricot	9–yellow	17–white
2–brown	10–green	18–gray
3–red	11–forest green	19–red violet
4–turquoise blue	12–orchid	20–violet red
5–blue	13–violet (purple)	21–tickle me pink
6–goldenrod	14–blue violet	22–red orange
7–black	15–macaroni & cheese	23–green yellow
8–robin's egg blue	16–orange	24–yellow green

Feast of the Immaculate Conception—December 8

From the very first moment of her life, Mary was free from original sin. On the Feast of the Immaculate Conception we celebrate this special grace and privilege God gave Mary because he had chosen her to be the mother of his Son.

Christmas—December 25

Jesus, the Son of God, was born in a place where animals were sheltered. His mother Mary and his foster father Joseph were poor. Simple shepherds were the first people to adore him. On Christmas we celebrate because the Son of God became man to save us from sin and death. When Jesus fills our lives and our hearts, the joy of Christmas can last all year long!

Feast of the Holy Family—the Sunday after Christmas*

Jesus wanted to grow up like we do—in a family. On this feast we celebrate the family into which Jesus was born. Jesus, his mother Mary, and his foster father Joseph, always did what God wanted them to do. This is why we call them the *Holy Family*.

*When Christmas is on a Sunday, this feast is celebrated on December 30.

Feast of Mary, Mother of God—January 1

Eight days after Christmas, the Church honors Mary. Her son Jesus is truly God the Father's eternal Son, the second person of the Holy Trinity. This is why Mary really is the Mother of God. This feast helps us to remember how great Jesus our Savior is and how special his mother Mary is.

Feast of the Epiphany—the Sunday between January 2 and January 8*

On the Feast of the Epiphany we remember the time when three wise men from far off lands came to adore Jesus and give him gifts. They brought him gold because Jesus is a King, frankincense because he is God, and myrrh because he would one day suffer. This feast teaches us that Jesus came to bring salvation to everyone.

*In countries where it is a holy day of obligation, Epiphany is celebrated on January 6.

Feast of the Baptism of the Lord—the Sunday after January 6

Before he began to preach, Jesus was baptized by his cousin John in the Jordan River. As Jesus came up out of the water, the Holy Spirit came down over him in the form of a dove. Then God the Father's voice was heard saying: "This is my beloved Son. I am pleased with him."

Feast of the Conversion of St. Paul—January 25

As a young man, Paul was called Saul. He hated Christians and tried to kill them. He didn't know any better. Once when he was on his way to arrest some Christians, the risen Jesus appeared to him. Jesus asked, "Saul, Saul, why are you persecuting me?" Saul realized he was hurting Jesus when he hurt the Christians. He had a *conversion* (a change of heart). From then on Saul used his new name, Paul, and he loved Jesus very much.

Feast of the Presentation of the Lord—February 2

Forty days after Christmas the Church remembers the day Mary and Joseph presented Jesus in the Temple of Jerusalem, according to the Law of the Jewish religion. An old man named Simeon and a widow named Anna were there. God let them recognize Jesus as the Messiah. Simeon and Anna were very happy to see Jesus.

St. Patrick—March 17

St. Patrick, the great apostle of Ireland, was born in Great Britain around the year 385. Patrick was kidnapped by Irish pirates and grew up as a slave in Ireland. Finally he escaped back to England and became a priest. Later he returned to Ireland to teach the Irish people about Jesus. Since Patrick's death, missionaries from Ireland have traveled all over the world.

Feast of the Annunciation—March 25

"Annunciation" means the telling or announcing of something. This feast celebrates the day on which the Archangel Gabriel brought a special message from God to Mary. The angel told Mary that God wanted her to be the mother of his Son. Mary wanted to do whatever God wished. She said "Yes" to the angel.

Passion Sunday, also called Palm Sunday

On Palm Sunday, we begin Holy Week. We remember the time Jesus entered the city of Jerusalem riding on a donkey. Many children and poor people surrounded him crying out, "Hosanna!" and waving palm branches. Children and the poor were always Jesus' favorites. Just a few days after this event, Jesus would offer his life for us on Calvary.

Good Friday—the Friday after Palm Sunday

On this day we remember in a special way that Jesus suffered and died on the cross to save us from our sins. We thank Jesus for loving us so much and we offer him all our love in return.

Easter Sunday—the Feast of the Resurrection

Easter is the *greatest* feast of the Church. On this Sunday we celebrate because Jesus, who gave his life for us on the cross and died for our sins, was raised from the dead! Jesus is alive and always with us. One day we will go to live with him in heaven!

World Day of Prayer for Vocations—Fourth Sunday of Easter

On this Sunday the Gospel reminds us that Jesus, our Good Shepherd, is always watching over us with love and care. On this day we pray in a special way for those men and women whom God is calling to become priests, brothers and sisters in his Church. Priests, brothers and sisters try to care for all God's people like Jesus the Good Shepherd.

Feast of St. Joseph the Worker—May 1

Joseph, the foster father of Jesus, was a carpenter. On this feast we honor St. Joseph and we think about the value of work. Everyone has to do some kind of work. We can use our talents to give praise to God when we work. Our work can be holy!

Feast of the Ascension—forty days after Easter,
or in some western dioceses, the following Sunday

On the Feast of the Ascension we celebrate the day the risen Jesus returned in glory to his Father in heaven. On that day, Jesus promised that he would be with us always—even until the end of the world!

Feast of Pentecost—the Sunday that comes seven weeks after Easter

About fifty days after Easter as Mary and the Apostles were praying together, the Holy Spirit came down upon them in the form of tongues of fire. The Holy Spirit made them strong and filled them with God's gifts. The Holy Spirit makes us strong and fills us with God's gifts too!

Feast of the Holy Trinity—the Sunday after Pentecost

We believe in only one God in three divine Persons: the almighty Father, his only Son, and the Holy Spirit. We call this mystery of one God in three Persons the Most Holy Trinity. Each time we make the sign of the cross we make an act of faith in the Holy Trinity. Through God's love, we share in the life of the Trinity!

Feast of the Body and Blood of Christ—in the United States, the Sunday after Trinity Sunday

The Church sets aside a day each year to give special thanks for the Eucharist. This feast came to be called "Corpus Christi," which is Latin for "Body of Christ." We receive the Body and Blood of Christ in Holy Communion, and we adore him present in the Blessed Sacrament. We rejoice that Jesus is with us always in this sacrament.

Feast of the Sacred Heart of Jesus—the Friday following the
second Sunday after Pentecost

This feast reminds us of Jesus' great love for us. Celebrating the first Friday of every month or making a holy hour of prayer in honor of Jesus' Sacred Heart are ways to show our love for Jesus and to ask pardon for those people who do not accept his love.

Feast of St. Peter and St. Paul—June 29

Peter and Paul were great friends of Jesus. Jesus chose Peter to be the rock on which he would build his Church. Jesus chose Paul to travel around the world and tell all people about him. Both Peter and Paul were apostles and martyrs who died for Jesus in Rome.

Feast of the Transfiguration—August 6

Jesus' Transfiguration took place on a high mountain when he was with Peter, James, and John. His face and clothes became dazzling with light. God the Father's voice was heard saying: "This is my Son, listen to him!" At the Transfiguration Jesus showed his divine glory and prepared his closest apostles for his coming suffering and death.

Feast of Mary's Assumption into Heaven—August 15

On the Feast of the Assumption we celebrate the day when God took Mary, Jesus' mother, body and soul into heaven. Mary is very happy with Jesus in heaven. From heaven she prays for all of us.

Feast of the Birth of Mary—September 8

On this day we celebrate Mary's birthday. Mary is very special because God chose her to be the mother of his Son, Jesus. A very old tradition in the Church tells us that Mary's parents were St. Ann and St. Joachim.

Feast of the Guardian Angels—October 2

God has given each one of us a guardian angel to watch over us all during our life. This angel helps us to know what is right and wrong. Our angel loves us and wants to keep us close to God.

Feast of All Saints—November 1

Saints are God's special friends. Everyone who is in heaven is a saint. Do you know someone who loved God very much, and who is now in heaven with God? That person is a saint! Every year we have a special day to honor all the friends of God who are with him in heaven. We call it All Saints Day.

All Souls Day—November 2

On this special day we remember everyone who has ever lived and died in the world. We pray for our relatives and friends, our ancestors, and also for those people whom we don't know. We ask God to give them happiness and peace in their new life with him.

Feast of Christ the King—the last Sunday of November

On the last Sunday of the Church's year, we celebrate the Feast of Christ the King. Jesus is King of the whole universe because he has conquered sin and death. Jesus, our loving King, will rule forever!

BOOKS & MEDIA

The Daughters of St. Paul operate book and media centers at the following addresses. Visit, call or write the one nearest you today, or find us on the World Wide Web, www.pauline.org

CALIFORNIA
3908 Sepulveda Blvd., Culver City, CA 90230; 310-397-8676
5945 Balboa Ave., San Diego, CA 92111; 619-565-9181
46 Geary Street, San Francisco, CA 94108; 415-781-5180

FLORIDA
145 S.W. 107th Ave., Miami, FL 33174; 305-559-6715

HAWAII
1143 Bishop Street, Honolulu, HI 96813; 808-521-2731
Neighbor Islands call: 800-259-8463

ILLINOIS
172 North Michigan Ave., Chicago, IL 60601; 312-346-4228

LOUISIANA
4403 Veterans Memorial Blvd., Metairie, LA 70006; 504-887-7631

MASSACHUSETTS
Rte. 1, 885 Providence Hwy., Dedham, MA 02026; 781-326-5385

MISSOURI
9804 Watson Rd., St. Louis, MO 63126; 314-965-3512

NEW JERSEY
561 U.S . Route 1, Wick Plaza, Edison, NJ 08817; 732-572-1200

NEW YORK
150 East 52nd Street, New York, NY 10022; 212-754-1110
78 Fort Place, Staten Island, NY 10301; 718-447-5071

OHIO
2105 Ontario Street (at Prospect Ave.), Cleveland, OH 44115; 216-621-9427

PENNSYLVANIA
9171-A Roosevelt Blvd., Philadelphia, PA 19114; 215-676-9494

SOUTH CAROLINA
243 King Street, Charleston, SC 29401; 843-577-0175

TENNESSEE
4811 Poplar Ave., Memphis, TN 38117; 901-761-2987

TEXAS
114 Main Plaza, San Antonio, TX 78205; 210-224-8101

VIRGINIA
1025 King Street, Alexandria, VA 22314; 703-549-3806

CANADA
3022 Dufferin Street, Toronto, Ontario, Canada M6B 3T5; 416-781-9131
1155 Yonge Street, Toronto, Ontario, Canada M4T 1W2; 416-934-3440

¡También somos su fuente para libros, videos y música en Español!